TAKE
THE TIME
IT TAKES

MW00639892

Gospel Rescue Mission
" 2024 "

TAKE THE TIME IT TAKES

GOD Bless Us All !

AARON P. SCOTT

Take the Time it Takes
by Aaron P. Scott
© 2020 by Aaron P. Scott

All rights reserved.

Edited by Adam Colwell's WriteWorks, LLC: Adam Colwell
 and Ginger Colwell
Cover Design by Jaime Anaya
Typesetting by Katherine Lloyd, The DESK
Published by The Good Brothers Foundation

Printed in the United States of America

Print ISBN: 978-1-7356969-4-2
eBook ISBN: 978-1-7356969-5-9

CONTENTS

FOREWORD

Aaron Wyche, Creative Director,
The Good Brothers Foundation
and
David Kamara, Founder,
The Good Brothers Foundation

To the reader (From Aaron Wyche):

Take a moment to count your blessings for the journey you are on. Your life is destined for greatness. To read this and share it with my brother, Aaron P. Scott, someone who has helped me through so much, fills my heart with gratitude.

When I read a book, I take as much time as needed to thoroughly digest the food for thought that I am blessed to consume. This approach helps me gain a better understanding of the overall themes and messages being delivered. It allows me to fully assess the material and apply what I've learned in an effective manner.

Take the Time it Takes is a testament to the fact that change is constant. Until your last breath, you will always be changing in one way or another. It's inevitable. As I read this book, I was reminded that while change is inevitable, growth is a choice. The Good Brothers Foundation invites young men to make a choice: choose to grow.

To the reader (From David Kamara):

Engaging with this material was an empowering experience. Reading the excerpts that I was around for and saw firsthand took me back through those moments like they were yesterday. This is truly a coming of age story that enlightens and reminds us that we are made by the things we go through.

Being able to say that my brother lives what he is depicting and encouraging others to do is a Godsend. I credit Aaron for helping me rejoin my place in the walk with God. He has inspired me to write about my life and break through comfort zones to become who God created me to be. Aaron was the definition of what a brother is and embodies the traits of a true friend.

The Good Brothers Foundation was designed to lead young men toward their destiny and fulfilling their purpose. I hope many others get a chance to be a part of what the good brothers are doing. I recommend this book to every young man in the world and to any parent, teacher, or mentor in search of a way to reach young men and help them grow to overcome the obstacles of their destiny.

To the author:

Good brother, it was amazing to read how you incorporated your personal journey into this book, and I believe your readers will feel the same. We go way back, and being able to watch you overcome the obstacles of your destiny has always been an inspiration to me. But to see you putting it on paper for the world to see takes heart, courage, and love. It takes *everything*. By being transparent about your personal struggles and reflecting on how you pulled through, you will help your readers connect to their own stories.

God left you here for a reason: to teach young men how to grow to overcome their obstacles of their destiny and become the men God created them to be.

Author's Note

This book is written to be conversational.
Therefore, proper grammar or sentence structure
is not always observed, and that is intentional.

PREFACE

Grace and peace, Good Brother! Welcome. I'm so excited you're here, man. Whether you realize it or not, you have overcome a great deal already just to be here, and I praise God for that. I praise God for you. Maybe you've never had someone tell you that before—or, if you have, perhaps it's been a while. Either way, I mean it from the bottom of my heart.

So, now what? Well, the fact that you picked this up tells me that you are ready for something new. You are starting to learn some things, and you want to build on what you know to get the next level. I've been there. I remember asking myself, "How do I do it?" "How do I use my past to help me press into my future?"

I wrote *Take the Time it Takes* to help you explore those questions. I wrote it to educate you. I wrote it to empower you. Think of it as a bridge or a toolkit to help you get from where you are to where you want to be.

For those of you who are doubtful or anxious about taking this step, that's okay. Just know, if you want to see change in your life, and you are willing to do whatever it takes, then you can achieve your goals. You can transform your life. You can turn your dreams into reality.

You might be saying, "Yeah, yeah, I've heard that before. Whatever, man, you don't know me." You're right. I don't. But based on my own life, and years of working with young men just like you, I've seen how broken families, a poor educational system, and institutionalized racism can leave one feeling marginalized and victimized. I've witnessed what incarceration and joblessness can do to a person to undermine their physical, emotional, and spiritual well-being. I've experienced what it's like to have a major setback and then have to figure out a way to turn a mess into a masterpiece.

That's why I wrote this. To share what the Lord has revealed to me. I've experienced the hard feelings, and I found a way to free myself from the places where I feel I've been let down or that I've I messed up. God showed me how to transform the way I think and how to grow to overcome the obstacles of my destiny. I'm writing this to you as a remnant of those who have gone before me, and a beacon to those who will follow. Those are the three enduring characteristics of The Good Brothers Foundation : transformation, growth, and legacy. Be encouraged, brother. You can do these things, too.

Let's set a few things straight. This isn't about denying your past or your present. Stuff is not going good at school. Your teachers or other adults had low expectations for you. Your family members aren't the best role models. Somehow you are not getting the love and support you need. Maybe you've seen or endured some kind of abuse or neglect. Perhaps you've just made some bad decisions. You had things going for you, but you messed them up. At whatever level it was for you, those were your realities. But it's like that old adage says, "Whatever doesn't kill you makes you stronger." We are made by the things we go through—and what you go through isn't just about you. It adds to your story, so that one day you can help someone like you. You are not the only one. There is nothing new under the sun. The way I see you, Good Brother, not only did you survive, you thrived to the point where you are today. So, don't deny your past. Take it and use it to press forward. Your current challenges are nothing compared to the greatness that will be revealed in you.

Know this, brother. You will be treated based upon your behavior, your actions and reactions. You will be handled in accordance with the presence that you bring into any given situation and with the contributions that you add to any given circumstance. How you handle problems and your perspective on them will determine what you achieve. The great thing is you have far more control over your destiny than you give yourself credit for. That's a fact!

Are you excited? Challenged? Curious? I hope it's a little bit of all of that as we begin to crack open this toolkit together. In *Take the Time it Takes*, we are going to learn about principles, fundamental truths that serve as a foundation for you to transform your thinking. These principles have numerous applications in every dimension of your life, and as you practice and apply them, you will grow mentally, emotionally, socially, physically, and spiritually:

- Sowing and Reaping – I get out what I put in
- Discovering Balance – The noun and the verb
- Developing Leadership – Decisions are made by those who show up
- Patience – Take the time it takes, and it will take less time
- Good Brothers – Do it for the culture
- Becoming a Godly Man – A part of society, but apart from it
- Creating a Legacy – Be faithful

INTRODUCTION

Born in New Jersey in 1985, I am the oldest of two boys and come from interracial parents. My dad was black, also grew up in Jersey, and came from an abusive background. He told my brother and me about how he and his five brothers and one sister lived in terror their entire childhood.

One story was especially scary. It happened when his father, a construction worker, was building their house and had the boys help him on the job. My dad, who was 10 years old, said they couldn't make a single mistake. If they so much as drove a nail the wrong way, my dad was afraid he or his siblings were going to be hurt by their father. On this day, my dad was chasing his four-year-old brother around the yard. The brother was screaming as my dad tried to catch him, but this moment of play was intolerable to his father. Enraged, he took the hatchet he was using to chop some wood and hurled it at my dad, hitting him on the back of the head, cracking his head wide open, and knocking him out cold. To this day, my dad still has a bald spot where the hatchet struck.

Apparently, such physical abuse was typical. In addition, as I'm sure you can imagine, my dad said his upbringing was super strict. He wasn't allowed to have friends or be involved in any after-school activities like sports or clubs. Dad was never told why. His father wasn't the type to break anything down like that. It was just, "Because I said so." It was a rigid, controlling home founded on and festering in fear.

My mom was white, grew up in Queens, New York, and was raised in an entirely opposite type of home. Her father was an executive; her mother was a stay-at-home mom. The oldest of three, my mom's home did not have any abuse, but it did know heartache: her father passed away when she was a young adult. I never got to know him, but I wish I had. My mom ended up the first of her family to attend college. That's where my parents met—in the late 1970s at what is now William Paterson University. They were both in nursing school there and though they shared the college experience, they came from divergent backgrounds, and therefore, had different perspectives on how to run a family.

The religious heritages of my parents are interesting. My mom's grandmother fled Poland during the Holocaust of World War II—meaning she was Jewish, even though my mom, to my knowledge, never formally practiced Judaism. Meanwhile, my dad's grandfather was a pastor. Growing up, he and his family went to my great grandfather's church. I learned early that faith doesn't make me who I am until I decide to make my faith a *part* of who I am through an authentic, active relationship with God.

My mom and dad got married in 1982, and I was born three years later. My dad was an alcoholic for the first seven years of my life. It was his coping mechanism of choice as he tried to deal with the abuse he suffered as a child and the brokenness and sense of isolation it bred inside of him. He excelled as a nurse, working in the cardiac units of hospitals before eventually becoming a clinical engineer for a medical device manufacturing company. When I was a small boy, my dad was harsh with me verbally, emotionally, and physically, though it was nowhere near what he endured as a child. He was angry and irritated most of the time. There was a constant edge to him. If he got mad, he could blow up quickly.

Usually when I was punished, I got spanked. It never felt like he abused us. We were just brought up in a home where discipline was physically administered.

I countered my dad by being strong-willed and stubborn with him, which, of course, often got me in trouble. Those difficult early years also contributed to some significant emotional, behavioral, and mental health issues later in my upbringing. Yet I saw my dad as being strong and consistent. Yes, he was mad, but he was that way all the time, so I knew what I was dealing with. He drew a line and didn't budge. I bucked against it, but I also respected it—and gradually began respecting *him*, starting with his decision to give up alcohol. He came to a point where he realized it was destroying him and hurting his family. He decided to take a stand, put the alcohol aside, and become the man he wanted to be, one who prioritized caring for his family ahead of everything else. He never drank again.

That change coincided with his decision to repent and obey God. He participated in various support and prayer groups as well as Alcoholics Anonymous. Even as a young boy, he talked to me about working through the 12 steps to recovery and always brought it back around to God's grace. "By the grace of God," he said time and again. As his faith changed who he was, he taught me moral principles. He taught me to respect authority, not do drugs, and not have sex before marriage.

> "By the grace of God," he said time and again.

That messaging was solid and constant. He believed in it with all his heart, as did my mom. She started out as a pediatric nurse, but after my brother and I were born, she said it was too heartbreaking for her to continue to care for sick babies. She started caring for adults and eventually began doing hospice care. Her career reflected her nurturing nature that she displayed in our home. She was always there for us, always supportive, always caring, and always affirming. She told my brother and me that we were handsome, smart, athletic, and could do anything we set our minds to do. She championed our involvement in extracurricular activities. Of course, she struggled with my dad through his recovery, but their relationship improved when they began to acknowledge God in all their ways rather than leaning on their own understanding.

She taught me many things. One of her favorite sayings was, "*Take the time it takes*, and it will take less time." She also spoke of "growth angels," which she defined as people or circumstances that come into our lives to challenge us. Mom said they were growth angels because they caused us to dig deep and use all our resources to discover how to deal with the person or situation. Mom's positive, moral-based interaction was encouraging to me and my brother. I was two-and-a-half years older than him and we were quite different from each other. As kids, I tended to go outside and play with others in the neighborhood, while he preferred to stay inside and build things with his Legos and play video games. I was the extrovert; he was much more the introvert. He was also tremendously creative and incredibly studious. He went on to go into the United States Navy as a nuclear engineer. I saw him as a rock star. The strong silent type. He didn't talk much, but when he did, people listened.

Despite the influence Christianity had in our home, I was negatively affected by my dad's angry, alcoholic years when I was a small boy. In the same way I once opposed my father's discipline at home, I started acting out in school. I was the class clown, ever ready to get everybody riled up and laughing about something. Whenever my behavior was corrected by a teacher, I'd just find ways to make things worse. In time, my defiance and unruly behavior caused me to be tagged as socially and emotionally disturbed. They said I had attention deficit disorder, and my dad was convinced that I was completely incorrigible. I was eventually placed into a special education classroom. At the same time, I was smart and placed in enrichment classes, where I worked on problem solving, critical thinking, creative group projects, and leadership development. So, I was intelligent yet rebellious. I was on top of whatever task or assignment I received and finished it quickly, and then I was off running amok, having fun, and sometimes even leaving the classroom without permission.

My teachers didn't know what to do with me. No one did.

■——■

As I entered my teen years, it only got worse. In middle school, I started smoking marijuana. The first time I tried it, I didn't get high and was so unimpressed with the experience that I told my buddy who offered it to me I had to call my parents to tell them what I did—not to get him in trouble, but simply to come clean.

"If I tell them," I said, "they will forgive me. I'll probably get in trouble, but it'll be okay."

My friend, who was higher than a skyscraper, responded, "No, man, don't tell 'em. They don't need to know."

I thought about it. *What they don't know won't hurt them.* "Alright. Fine."

That was a turning point. My decision to hide what I was doing from my parents made it easier the next time—and the next. Before I knew it, I was getting high almost every day and enjoying it. After marijuana, the dominoes started to fall. I began getting into other drugs. I did drugs to have fun and to help me take my mind off of things that I didn't want to think about. It definitely ended up hurting me more than it helped.

My drug use quickly led to other bad decisions and more secrets to conceal from my parents. I couldn't hide everything. I was arrested one night when I met up with some buddies in a field near the school to drink and get high. We got caught, and my dad had to come to the police station to pick me up. But even that incident didn't deter me. I started hanging out with drug dealers and observed that they were making money—so I started dealing. As the cash came in, my pride grew. I started robbing people and getting into fights. I was definitely headed down the wrong road, and I kept all of this hidden from my parents and little brother. They had no idea what I was becoming.

That is, until the one day I called my dad from school and asked him to drop off some soccer equipment I needed for practice. He went into my room in the basement of our home, and as he searched for the gear, he also found my drug stash; specifically, marijuana and a pipe. It wasn't much, but it was enough to prompt him to call the police. It turned out he had already suspected me of doing drugs, had contacted them before, and was told to get back in touch with them if he found evidence. I guess I wasn't fooling my family as well as I thought I was.

He brought me my soccer stuff but said nothing about his discovery. I ended up being out all weekend partying with my friends and didn't come home until Sunday. I walked in, planning to be home just long enough to change clothes and head out again.

"Hey, son," he opened. "Where have you been?"

"I've been out with my boys," I said, not wanting to divulge any more, "and I'm leaving again. I just came home to—"

"You haven't been home all weekend," he interrupted.

"I'm not a little boy, dad," I said, now getting aggravated. "I can do what I want when I want."

"You can, huh?" he responded, then reached behind a shelf

next to him to reveal my stash. He held it out in front of him. "You mean like this? What is all this?"

Of course, the question was rhetorical. He knew what it was and why I had it.

"Why are you going through my stuff?" I responded, a heightened edge in my voice.

"I wasn't looking for it," he countered, glaring at me. "But I found it when I was looking for your soccer stuff."

I stepped forward and started toward him. "Well, give it back!"

I tried to grab it, but he wrestled himself away, instantly got out his phone, and called the police. In my arrogance, though, I wasn't worried. *What are the cops going to do about a little marijuana?* I mused. *Nothing is going to happen.* I chilled on the sofa until they arrived.

Two officers walked in, and my father showed them what he had found. Next thing I knew, I was being handcuffed, led outside, and put into the back of a paddy wagon. It all happened so fast I hardly knew what to think.

I plopped down on the hard and uncomfortable bench with my arms and hands confined behind me. There were no windows. As I bounced with the movement of the van, I thought to myself, *This is all new to me. I have no idea what's going to happen next.* It was weird, and I was scared at the unknown.

When we arrived, I was directed out of the vehicle and saw I was at a juvenile detention center. While I was processed, I learned it operated by a tiered system. The longer you were there and the better you behaved, the more privileges you received. Since I was a new resident, I was at the lowest tier of everything. My earlier anticipation quickly faded.

I was then shown to my bunk, a small space among six that

lined each side of a common area in the center. The cinder block room had a low steel shelf that protruded from the wall. It served as my bed and was equipped with a half-inch thick pad and a thin blanket. It didn't have a pillow. There was no desk. No nightstand. No toilet. The bathroom area was separate and shared by everyone. The only other item in the room was a single, exposed light bulb in the ceiling.

For the next two weeks, that room was my home—and the daily routine never changed. There were set times for waking up, showering, and eating. Group counseling and support sessions took place between meals, as did brief times for physical or recreational activity. You always ended up back in your bunk. I was so angry I'd get on the phone with my parents and cuss them out. I was harsh. But the people at the detention center quickly impressed upon me that it was my responsibility to get myself straightened out. Early in my time there, I remember a specific conversation with a staff member. He asked me to tell him my story, and I told him what I was into, what I'd been doing, and how I'd got there. He then challenged, "Are you going to do that for the rest of your life?" I'd never looked at it that way before. It definitely put things in perspective. I didn't have an answer that very moment, but I sure thought about it the rest of the time I was there. *Is this really what I am going to do? Rob people? Do drugs? Fight? Get in trouble?*

Is this my life?

When I was released, I was taken back home and placed on probation. I went to work in a shoe store as part of my restitution, and I also had to go to drug counseling. I got clean—for a while. It was nice to be sober and have a clear mind. It was the first time I came up for air and recognized I might have other options for my life. But before long, I started to slip back into old habits. Despite everything that happened, I hadn't changed my mindset.

Understandably, this frustrated my parents, especially dad. He began to think there was nothing he could do for me. Still, he devoted himself to prayer and, I'd later learn, chose to trust God to deal with me because everything he had tried to do in his own strength to help me didn't seem to be working.

> I couldn't quite explain it, but I knew there was something more.

For a few more months, I returned to my party-driven, drug-induced routine. I thought I had it all. Money. Girls. Respect.

But the words I heard in juvie wouldn't leave my mind. "Are you going to do that for the rest of your life?"

Inside, a voice started crying out. *What are you doing? You don't belong with these guys? They aren't on your level.*

You're better than this.

You know you are.

I couldn't quite explain it, but I knew there was something more. I'd have these moments of clarity where I saw what I could become—should become.

It was during these brief instances that I'd remember back to a moment when I was five years old, sitting with my mother in the kitchen one Sunday afternoon after church. I said to her, "Mom, I want to ask Jesus to come into my heart." That was the subject of the Sunday school class that day. As she prayed with me, I looked over at a picture on the wall. It depicted Jesus knocking on a door—and in my mind, as she prayed, I saw Jesus literally knocking on the door of my heart, the door opening, and Him entering it. I know that it actually happened. It was such a vivid memory, so real.

Then I'd come back to reality, laying on my bed at home after another night of partying, and I'd ask God to forgive me yet again.

■ ·— —·■

In the end, I decided the way I was living just wasn't worth the bother. I had no business selling drugs. It just wasn't right, and there was too much risk. I also realized I was growing up—about to leave high school and become a man, and I needed to act like it. When I was sober, there was a substantial and positive difference in my mood, attitude, and fitness. I got along with others better. Most importantly, my relationship with my parents not only improved, but stabilized. There was no more fighting or arguing, no more disrespect by me toward them—especially my father. By the grace of God, we had started down a path of restoration that continued in the years ahead.

Finally, as things became right with my mother and father, I began to look toward my future and the potential of someday having my own family that I could lead the way I wanted to. It wasn't that my parents had done things poorly with me. They hadn't. But I did start getting an idea of doing things differently than them. I wasn't exactly sure what that meant—but I sure wasn't going to find out if I kept living the way I was.

I chose to leave behind the old life and head off to college. To make a fresh start.

Yet I still had a lot to learn.

1

SOWING AND REAPING

*Don't be misled: No one makes a fool of God. What a person
plants, he will harvest. The person who plants selfishness, ignoring
the needs of others—ignoring God!—harvests a crop of weeds.
All he'll have to show for his life is weeds! But the one who plants
in response to God, letting God's Spirit do the growth work in him,
harvests a crop of real life, eternal life. So let's not allow
ourselves to get fatigued doing good. At the right time we
will harvest a good crop if we don't give up, or quit.*
(GALATIANS 6:7-9, MSG)

I get out what I put in.

There is something happening in you, and to you, all the time.
From the moment you are born until you breathe your last
breath, it never stops. Whether you are aware of it or not, this
truth is impacting your life. It is a law as certain as the gravity that
holds you on the ground.

You reap what you sow—or, more simply put, you get out
what you put in.

Every moment of every day, you are sowing into your life. Be it your faith, your relationships, your wisdom and knowledge, or even your physical health and strength, you are determining your present and creating your future with each decision you make.

This is what you *sow* or put in.

Yet every one of those choices will have different outcomes. They will be good, or they will be bad, but they will occur.

This is what you *reap* or get out.

Therefore, since you are always sowing into your life, there is a very important question you must ask yourself:

What am I sowing into my life?

The answer is vital because what you sow determines what you reap.

Jesus taught a lesson about sowing and reaping. It teaches us about people that sow his words into their lives.

They are like a man building a house, who dug down deep and laid the foundation on rock. When a flood came, the torrent struck that house but could not shake it, because it was well built. But the one who hears my words and does not put them into practice is like a man who built a house on the ground without a foundation. The moment the torrent struck that house, it collapsed, and its destruction was complete. (Luke 6:48-49)

When you sow God's Word into your life, then by God's grace you will be able to stand strong and overcome any obstacle you face.

By the time I started classes at Bucks County Community

College just outside Philadelphia,]
that I wanted more out of my life th
I was making better decisions than
still really didn't know what I wan
becoming a teacher, but I just wa
work quickly so that I could get c
life. I was in a hurry, and I didn
should've.

My freshman year, I picked something I liked—health and
physical education—and I started working toward it. The first two
years, things went well. Then I transferred to a four-year university. It was exciting and came with a lot more opportunity. There
were so many different things to do, and I made a lot of friends. I
got involved in different clubs, groups, student government, and
peer education. I even pledged for a fraternity. But I took on too
much at once, and my grades began to suffer. I changed my major,
hoping to salvage a few good grades and make the best out of the
situation, but I was still rushing.

I was like the man who built his house without a foundation.
I knew college was important, but I simply didn't *take the time it
takes* to figure out how to build a solid foundation for my goals. I
didn't realize that college was much more than just the end of
my school days. It was a special time of preparation for the next
chapter in my life. I didn't *take the time it takes* to explore and
develop my gifts or interests. I just jumped from one opportunity
to the next.

Even though I wasn't as focused and intentional as I could
have been, God was still faithful. While I was busy rushing
through my life in college, God revealed to me that He created
me with a desire to help people, especially my brothers, build
strong spiritual foundations by teaching and modeling principles

that would help them grow to overcome the obsta-
destiny.

he same time, I had found my own destiny.

began to study God's Word and apply it to my schoolwork
d my relationships with family and friends. Before long, I was
growing more than I could've asked or imagined. Then came an
unexpected setback. I was working at night as a valet driver in
Philadelphia and had just gotten off work. With a pocket full of tip
money, I was on the phone making plans with a friend as I walked
toward the Broad Street subway. In the midst of our conversation,
I had to move out of the way of a person riding by me on a bike.

I kept walking and talking until, moments later, I crossed by
the entrance to an alley.

"Hey! Get off the phone!"

I turned around in the direction of the voice, and a person
stepped out of the shadows with a gun at his hip. It was pointed
right at me.

I didn't throw my hands up and say, "Don't shoot!" Instead, I
lowered the hand holding the phone while holding my other arm
in an outstretched motion, my hand pressing downward. "Whoa,
calm down. Let's—"

"POP!" He fired the weapon, and I felt the bullet enter my
abdomen, right next to my belly button.

I went down to one knee, not yet aware of any pain in the
shock of it all. "Do you want the phone now?" I asked him, grunt-
ing. It never occurred to me to offer him my money. He must've
been watching me, but I really don't think he meant to shoot me
or even planned to rob me. Otherwise, he would've demanded
my money right away.

Whatever the case, he quickly grabbed the phone, got on the
bike, and took off. That's when I realized it was the same cyclist I

had moved away from a minute earlier.

I hadn't hung up, and later my friend on the phone told me she didn't hear a gunshot, but only a rustling noise as if the phone had been put in someone's pocket. She did know, however, that I was in a dangerous neighborhood and assumed I was in trouble, so she got in her car and headed toward where she thought I was.

At the same time she was doing that, I laid down on the pavement. I was sure I was going to die, right there in the street.

That summer I'd been learning a lot in church about gratefulness. My first thought was, *God, thank you. Thank you for these 24 years.*

I didn't see a bright light or pearly gates. I didn't hear a trumpet announce my passage to the other side. But I did hear a quiet, still voice. It said four words.

"You can't stay here."

With that, I got up and ran as fast as I could, making my way to a Chinese food store a half block away. I stumbled inside and saw the wide-eyed clerk. "Help! I've been shot."

Even though I was clutching my stomach and there was blood all over my shirt, the store worker responded, "I can't understand you. I can't help." At the same time, a customer walked right by me as he left the store. I went to leave—and the next thing I knew a police officer was there. He explained later that he heard the shot and was circling around to see what happened. He picked me up, put me in the back of the car, and took me to the nearest hospital. Just after I was taken away, the girl I was talking to on the phone showed up and saw the cop cars and caution tape at the scene.

By the time I was stabilized and transported to Temple University Hospital, she had contacted my brother, who in turn got in touch with my mom. She found out where I had been taken and was there with my parents after I got out of surgery.

I was on the operating table for 20 hours and stayed in the hospital for 19 days. Mom, dad, my brother, and my friends visited often, even helping later with my rehabilitation. I had plenty of time to understand how close I had come to death, and it gave me a whole new perspective on life—and living. If God wanted to take me home, it seemed that would have been as good a time as any. But He didn't. I knew I had been left here for a reason.

My destiny.

When I returned to college, I decided to change my major back to education and focus on developing the skills I needed to pursue my destiny. I was determined to follow through and perhaps even help those like my gunman—young men on a path to destruction.

However, after just a couple semesters back, I exhausted all my financial aid. Out of money and unwilling to go further into debt, I left school and entered the workforce. My first job after college was as a sales associate at a shoe store.

I was 26 years old and not sure what was going to happen next. My destiny was still there, but it didn't feel like I was walking in it.

■ — — ■

Hopefully, your college experience will turn out differently—and better—than mine. Nevertheless, through it all, my experience taught me a great deal about sowing and reaping. On the negative side, I was too set in my own ways and didn't accept instruction. My hard-headedness was costly. I sowed obstinance and reaped ignorance that came from not listening. I also spent a lot of time and money on things I thought were cool at the time but were actually a waste. It was like I was pouring water into this big bucket that had a hole in the bottom. No matter how much I put in, none of it lasted. I sowed wastefulness in the name of having fun and reaped the lack of resources.

It's not all bad, though. There were three big positives that came out of my college years. First, I reaped adaptability as I sowed exploration that came with changing majors and participating in various clubs and activities. I may not necessarily have focused on one group, but I was focused on growing. I was devoted to learning as much as I could about anything that was related to my destiny.

During one summer job stint at an area community center, a gentleman said something to me I'll never forget. I asked him how he was doing one morning, and he responded, "I'm doing the best I can with what I got." That's the core of adaptability. When you learn something powerful, take it to heart—meditate on it, apply it to your life, and share it with others.

> When you learn something powerful, take it to heart— meditate on it, apply it to your life, and share it with others.

Second, I reaped insight as I sowed engagement that brought me in contact with a lot of different people. From the classroom to the dormitories and everywhere in between on and off campus, I experienced the good, the bad, and the ugly of college life. Through it all, I met so many kinds of people, and I learned something from every situation. I discovered things I could use to build upon and things that I did not want to perpetuate. The Bible says that all things are permissible, but not all things are beneficial (1 Corinthians 10:23). That means that you can do whatever you want, but the questions you should always ask yourself are, "Is this in alignment with my destiny?" and "Will this get me closer to my goal?"

Finally, as I sowed cooperation, I reaped leadership skills.

This was most apparent in my fraternity, Kappa Alpha Psi Fraternity, Inc. Our motto was, "Achievement in every field of human endeavor. Training for leadership since 1911." While we were a fraternity (and we did have our share of parties), the bar was set pretty high in terms of our involvement on campus.

I recall four fraternity brothers in particular. The first was always cracking jokes and goofing around. He seemed to counter anything I said, almost to the point of being adversarial, because he was so nonchalant and sarcastic. Yet when it was time for the work to get done, he was there. He brought an authenticity to our projects. The second was an athlete who, because of his status on the team, was given preferential treatment. It didn't seem he had to put in the same amount of work as the rest of us. That bothered me at first, but since he was somewhat of a celebrity on campus, he brought notoriety to our fraternity in a way that benefitted us all. The third had a huge personality, and it was contagious. While he was unpolished and some of his ideas were not fully thought out, he did wonders for our morale and brought such energy to our endeavors. Finally, the last brother was calm, diligent, and had built great relationships with administrators and other campus organizations. Even more, he orchestrated a lot of the behind-the-scenes work and kept everyone in the chapter engaged. He truly drove home the brotherhood aspect of our fraternity.

Serving with my brothers taught me how to adjust to others versus forcing them to adjust to me. It helped me to understand group dynamics and see how each member had a specific part to play, just like the Bible says in Ephesians 4:16.

From him the whole body, joined and held together by every supporting ligament, grows and builds itself up in love, as each part does its work.

This taught me how to be more accepting, forgiving, and loving toward others and myself when things did not go exactly as I thought they should. There were times I didn't get it exactly right, moments where I fell short of my own expectations—but I learned that the show must go on.

By the time I left school and launched into the workforce, I knew that the principle of sowing and reaping was undeniable. I can't stress this enough: it is always happening. Even better, you can *trust* this principle. Think of it? You can sow energy and reap growth. You can sow time and reap experience. You can sow concern and reap compassion. You can sow love and reap relationships. You can sow prayer and reap understanding. Whatever you sow you will reap—and you'll also find that when you begin to align yourself with others that are sowing like you, the harvest is magnified.

This principle is one of the keys to transforming your life.

Dear God, no one can make a fool of you. What I sow, I will reap. If I sow selfishness, ignoring the needs of others and ignoring you, I will not reap anything good. But if I sow in response to you, letting your Spirit work in me, I will reap good things. Give me strength, God, so that I don't grow tired of doing good. I will be like the man building a house, who dug down deep and laid the foundation on rock. When obstacles arise, they will not break me. Now, to you who are able to do immeasurably more than all I can ask or imagine, according to your power that is at work within me, to you be glory in the church and in Christ Jesus throughout all generations, forever and ever! Amen.

2

DISCOVERING BALANCE

Teach us to number our days,
that we may gain a heart of wisdom.

(PSALM 90:12)

The noun and the verb.

Stephen Curry is a National Basketball Association (NBA) champion and most valuable player (MVP) with the Golden State Warriors who many say is the greatest pure shooter to ever play the game. His quick release, smooth movement with or without the ball, and three-point shooting prowess are legendary. More than that, Stephen has been the recipient of the NBA Sportsmanship Award, supports numerous worthy charities, and is outspoken about his faith. He says he pounds his chest and points up during games to remind himself and others that he plays for God.[1]

In a game, he is uncanny at anticipating what his opponent is going to do and responding to it. In seconds, he assesses all of his options and finds a way to confuse the player guarding him.

He may go to the left or the right. He may pass or pump fake. He may use a crossover move or dribble the ball behind his back. Whatever it takes to get open and take the shot, Stephen makes it happen. Away from the arena, he maintains a well-balanced and healthy lifestyle that enables him to be productive and have a positive impact on those around him.

When we consider balance, we must understand that it is a noun and a verb. As a noun, balance has equal proportions and equal dimensions that counter one another to keep things in order. As a verb, balance becomes what we do, the *act* of making adjustments and aligning things so we don't do too much of one thing to the detriment of another.

As a young man, you are responsible for establishing and maintaining balance in your life. You are in control of how you prepare for and respond to life's challenges. Just like in basketball, you will come up against opposition in one way or another. Whether it's internal or external, obstacles will arise. Discovering balance will help you to overcome any obstacle you face.

In the end, it is up to you. That's a powerful truth—and also one that comes with a great deal of personal responsibility.

You may be wondering, "How do I discover balance?" Well, the first thing you have to do is look at the big picture. What is your goal? What do you want to reap? When we know what we want to get out, then we can think about what we have to put in. Next, you examine the various dimensions of health for your life: physical, emotional, mental, social, and spiritual. Let's take a deeper look at each one to have a better idea of what I'm talking about. From there, we can explore a few ways for you to optimize your schedule and adjust your environment to create balance in your life.

Physical health is critical and is the most visible of the various dimensions of health.[2] The condition of your body has an impact on how you deal with stress and go about making decisions. Your body is a machine, and just like any machine, it needs to be maintained. There are four main ways you maintain your body.

- Hygiene: Looking neat and smelling clean will make you feel better and present well to others. Well-kept hair and clean skin are less susceptible to viruses and bacteria. You will build a reputation with people based on how you present yourself to them each day.

- Diet: Your organs and tissues need proper nutrition to work effectively. In addition, what you eat will affect your mood, mental function, and performance. Fatty, sugary, and fast food choices have a negative impact on these things. Foods with too many chemicals and preservatives will drain your energy. Medical studies have shown a diet rich in fruits and vegetables not only make you feel better, but they may also reduce the risk of heart disease and even protect you from certain types of cancers.

- Exercise: Keeping a regular exercise regimen will make you healthy and fit, and it sends a positive message to others that you care about yourself. Not only does your fitness make you feel strong and confident, it will help you manage stress, accomplish daily tasks, and recover quickly from fatigue or injury.

- Rest: The idea of the "sabbath," or a day of rest, has been around since the beginning of time. Rest, and more specifically sleep, is paramount to your physical well-being. During sleep, physiological demands on your body are reduced and temperature and blood pressure drop. In general, brainwave activity, breathing, and heart rate are extremely regular when you are in deep sleep mode. This helps your body and mind recharge. Good sleep is fundamental. In fact, one study even asserted that one could survive for three times as long without food as one could without sleep.[3]

Emotional health is an important part of overall well-being. People who are emotionally healthy are in control of their thoughts, feelings, and behaviors.[4] As young men, this is an important time to develop emotional intelligence. Emotional intelligence is defined as the capability to:

- Recognize your own emotions
- Recognize the emotions of others
- Discern between different feelings and label them appropriately
- Use emotional information to guide thinking/behavior
- Manage or adjust emotions to adapt to environments/ achieve your goals

As you gain understanding about your emotions, you will be able to acknowledge them rather than suppress them or express them indiscriminately. Emotional intelligence empowers you to rule your emotions and not be ruled by them. I love the saying attributed to Martin Luther, the sixteenth-century theologian and monk who spearheaded the Protestant Reformation: "I can't stop a bird from flying over my head, but I can stop it from resting there."

Likewise, I can't stop an emotion from rising up within me, but I can control what I do about it when it does.

Mental health is defined as a state of well-being in which every individual realizes his potential, can cope with the normal stresses of life, can work productively, and is able to make a contribution to his community.[5] Proverbs 23:7 teaches us that as a man thinks within himself, so is he. This means in order to be overcomers, we must think like overcomers. Good Brothers was founded to transform the way young men think, but we can only help you transform if you are willing to be helped—and even then, you must grow by your own efforts.

Social health involves your ability to form satisfying interpersonal relationships with others. It also relates to your ability to adapt comfortably to different social situations and act appropriately in a variety of settings.[6] Some of the most satisfying relationships are found between like-minded people. Before you can find people who are like-minded, you have to define your own mind. How do you define your mind? That is a vital question—because your mindset will determine your social impact and strongly govern your balance in life. As you determine your mindset and core values, you will find a balance between what behaviors and attitudes you wish to minimize and those you want to maximize. That balance will make you a person of influence and it will help you create positive social change.

Spiritual health is defined by your values, principles, beliefs, and morals. Having compassion, the capacity for love and forgiveness, altruism, joy, and fulfillment help you enjoy your spiritual health.[7] When we deal with the spiritual, we deal with the invisible: things of faith. Faith is the substance of things hoped for, the evidence of things not seen (Hebrews 11:1). It can be hard to define, but when you find it, it brings balance and peace to your life that transcends all human understanding (Philippians 4:7).

You don't become an MVP overnight; just ask Steph. But if you *take the time it takes*, you'll get there. You will have to look at things from various perspectives, learn about your strengths and weaknesses, and find new strategies to manage your life. Most of all, this process demands resilience and grit. No matter how many times you get knocked down, you will get back up and keep setting your goals high. Why? Because it's worth it. It's worth going through the toil and the struggle, the troubles and the heartache—because once you find your balance, you'll experience an abundance of joy and peace. You will be wiser, and you will be in a position to lend your hope to those around you.

RHYTHM

Once you have achieved this sense of balance, the next step is to find a rhythm. I grew up listening to jazz music because my dad always listened to it. One of the best performers in the history of that great American music genre is Max Roach. A percussionist and composer, Max worked in a variety of styles but was a pioneer of bebop, a type of jazz characterized by complex harmonies, chord progressions, key changes, and rhythms. Among the techniques he introduced and evolved was the use of the cymbal instead of the bass drum to dictate the beat of a song. He played solos that mixed pitches and timbres using brushes as well as sticks. He notably played on Miles Davis' *Birth of the Cool* and collaborated in the groundbreaking *Freedom Now Suite*. He taught, composed, and recorded music until just a few years before his death in 2007 at the age of 83.

> Rhythm informs your life and generates a routine that can be adjusted as needed.

Musicians will tell you that what made Max one of a kind was what he did with rhythm to drive a song forward and provide prompts and space for the others on stage to improvise and pursue new heights on their own instruments. Max created the flow into which the other artists seamlessly entered and were enabled and emancipated to become stronger and more confident in their craft.

You need to find a rhythm that can give you the same kind of flow. Within flow you find flexibility, and within flexibility, freedom. Rhythm informs your life and generates a routine that can be adjusted as needed.

When you are intentional about all five dimensions of health, a rhythm will take shape and your life will move forward. Rhythm prevents frustration when things don't go according to plan. It doesn't give you control over everything, but it will help you get back on track when things happen. In the same way rhythm carries musicians to the end of the song, it will carry you to your destiny. The key is to stay focused on the vision and flexible on the details. Leadership expert, John C. Maxwell, talks about making critical decisions early and then managing them daily. Each situation that comes up requires you to make a decision. If that decision is not getting you closer to your destiny, then it is taking you away from it. The rhythm of your life helps to inform those decisions.

Where does this rhythm come from? I believe it goes back to what Stephen Curry has discovered: God. He is not only the creator of the rhythm, but He is the keeper of it as well, the heavenly Max Roach, who creates the beat of our lives. As we learn to keep pace with His beat, we'll not only pick up a routine for living, but others will start to notice it. Interestingly, quantum physicists have identified a scientific explanation to what is called "the law of attraction," the idea being that "knowingly or unknowingly, every second of our existence, we are acting as human magnets sending out our thoughts and emotions and attracting back more of what we have put out."[8] Some people say this shows that the "universe" is on our side. I believe this so-called "law of attraction" is actually a demonstration of God's faithfulness toward us.

TAKE THE TIME IT TAKES

Jesus taught us, "But seek first his kingdom and his righteousness, and all these things will be given to you as well." (Matthew 6:33)

When we are in step with God, we will be attractive to others because they are seeing Him in us. Even more, He will trust us with more as He sees that we are faithful with what He has given us.

As you learn to let God set the pace, you will begin to experience a sense of harmony between yourself and your surroundings. It doesn't mean things will be perfect all the time, but you'll start to see that in all things God works for the good of those who love Him and have been called according to His purpose (Romans 8:28). Everything will be moving toward your destiny together. You will establish a pattern of faithfulness by following God. A heavenly rhythm will bring blessings to you and cause you to be a blessing to others as you grow to overcome the obstacles of your destiny.

Dear God, you are balance. You do everything in a fitting and orderly way. Please teach me to number my days, so that I may gain wisdom and understanding. I approach your throne boldly and with confidence, as you have commanded me, so that I may receive mercy and find grace to help me in my time of need. I seek to establish and maintain balance in my life, but I seek first your kingdom and your righteousness, knowing that in you, all these things will be given to me as well. In Jesus' name, Amen.

3

DEVELOPING LEADERSHIP

Blessed is the one who perseveres under trial because,
having stood the test, that person will receive the crown of life
that the Lord has promised to those who love him.

(JAMES 1:12)

Decisions are made by those who show up.

"I say to you today, my friends, so even though we face the difficulties of today and tomorrow, I still have a dream. It is a dream deeply rooted in the American dream. I have a dream that one day this nation will rise up and live out the true meaning of its creed, 'We hold these truths to be self-evident, that all men are created equal.'"[9]

One of the greatest leaders this nation and world has ever known was Dr. Martin Luther King Jr. The above excerpt, from his speech at The March on Washington for Jobs and Freedom on August 28, 1963, will remain among the most famous words ever spoken.

But what many people don't know is that long before that speech was uttered, Dr. King led in the implementation of the Beloved Community, a group of people committed to and trained in the philosophy and methods of nonviolence (the cornerstone of his principles on nonviolence and "love in action" that were used by those involved in the civil rights movement of the 1950s-60s). They believed in a global vision where poverty, hunger, and homelessness were not to be tolerated because international standards of decency wouldn't allow it. Racism and all forms of discrimination and prejudice were also to be replaced by an all-inclusive spirit of brotherhood and sisterhood.

Dr. King certainly lived by my definition of leadership: helping people work together to accomplish a common goal. He did this by showing up, building relationships with others, seeking solutions, and working toward them. True leaders know how to empower others to act and keep them on course. This is difficult to do, but it is possible, especially when you understand what leadership is all about: relationships and adaptation. The impact Dr. King had on people was not about his titles. It was about his relationships: first with God and then with the people around him. When your leadership is driven by a divine calling, then God will be leading *through* you. When you turn to God for direction and strength, then you will be able to overcome any obstacle that gets in your way.

> When your leadership is driven by a divine calling, then God will be leading *through* you.

As 1 John 4:4 declares, *You, dear children, are from God and have overcome them, because the one who is in you is greater than the one who is in the world.*

I've identified four practical steps that will inspire you to relational leadership as a young man. Dr. King certainly demonstrated each one. You can, too.

1. Show up. I once heard it said, "Decisions are made by those who show up." Be in place and be "in the moment," fully present and fully engaged. Go to class. Go to the meeting. Go to work. Go support a friend's event, their performance, or their competition. Go to your family member's party, graduation, christening, or celebration. Be involved. Be supportive. Celebrate with people, standing by their side in the good and the bad. Just be there. Even if you didn't know how to help, just show up. Sometimes there is nothing you can do, but just being there makes a difference.

2. Be intentional. The spirit you bring to a situation will either help your team or hurt them. The Spirit of God within you is not one of fear, but of power, love, and self-control (2 Timothy 1:7). In developing your leadership, strive to think and speak like an overcomer, pushing yourself to stay positive even though you may not always feel that way. This will help you keep the faith that nothing can defeat you or your team.

Be intentional as well about building a reputation. Each interaction is an opportunity to create memories, set routines, and affect the thoughts and images that come into people's minds when they think about you. God will give you opportunities to show what you're made of, but what you *do* when those opportunities arise is up to you. Every decision you make has the potential to leave a lasting impression on those around you. Never underestimate the power of one interaction.

3. Go first. Lead from the front—doing, being, and living those things you hold in high esteem. Be the first to respond to a call to action. For example, when the teacher says it is time to start a group project, be the one that invites people into the group.

When you are in a meeting and the leader asks for a volunteer, raise your hand. When you are at the workplace and the boss needs someone to take the extra shift, be the one that picks up the slack. When a friend needs help moving, offer a helping hand. Going first is being a catalyst. A catalyst is the one that gets the ball rolling. The Good Brothers Foundation is about action. You be the icebreaker. You be the trailblazer. You be the risk taker. You go first. Be courageous. Do whatever it takes to get the job done, finding solutions, connecting to existing resources, and building new ones as needed.

4. Teach. Leaders with true power can step back and empower others to operate in their gifts. They invest in the people around them, and they serve through development and training. Realizing that they are being used by God to influence the people around them, they share their knowledge with humility to help others connect the dots between faith, growth, and advancement.

■ — — ■

These four concepts—show up, be intentional, go first, and teach—are good, but to have *great* impact with them, you must possess awareness. You must be cognizant of yourself, your team, and the goal. Maybe it is sensing when to step up and take charge or step back and create space for others to act. Perhaps it's figuring out how to inspire your team or measuring short-term progress in relationship to long-term goals. Your awareness will determine how you lead. The more aware you are, the better your leadership will be.

Here are some ways to gain awareness:

- Know what your desired outcome is and why
- Know what needs to be accomplished and have an action plan

- Know your strengths and areas of opportunity
- Know your limits and give 100 percent

Along with awareness comes adaptability. *Adaptive leadership,* just as the name suggests, requires you to adjust to whatever conditions you face. Compromise where you can, but where you can't, don't. It involves focus regarding the vision and flexibility regarding the details. Even more, it challenges you to be effective and efficient with the resources you

> Compromise where you can, but where you can't, don't.

have. Finding needs is easy. Filling them is the part that requires you to grow. Oftentimes, the resources you need are available, you just need to search for them.

> It is written, "Ask and it will be given to you; seek and you will find; knock and the door will be opened to you." (Matthew 7:7)

Don't be discouraged when you don't see the resources right away. Dig deep, keep searching, and do the best you can with what you've got.

Let's say you have a class project and you envision a video presentation that includes elaborate characters and scenes. You know you don't have money to hire actors, but guess what? You can get a couple of friends to play out your story, record it all on your phone, and download a free app to edit the video. That's an example of doing the best you can with what you've got. Such adaptability requires you to deconstruct your original thought and then reconstruct it into a feasible reality. This takes creativity, patience, resourcefulness, and persistence. These characteristics are present in every notable leader. They facilitate favorable outcomes and foster faithful followership.

> Luke 16:10 says, *Whoever can be trusted with very little can also be trusted with much, and whoever is dishonest with very little will also be dishonest with much.*

You may not be doing as much as you originally planned, but you are doing something—and you're making it work. In time, you will prove that you are trustworthy and diligent, and those around you will see that and gain confidence in you.

There are two essential "building" blocks to becoming an adaptive leader.

1. Building a team. Not everyone can do everything, but everyone can do something. You and each person on your team have different gifts (abilities that come naturally) and skills (abilities that are learned and developed). Each individual and ability is equally important to the execution of a goal. It calls to mind the funny saying, "If everyone stays in their lane and does the speed limit, there won't be any traffic." As an adaptive leader, one of your goals is to maximize the strengths of everyone around you.

You'll recall that my first job after college was as a sales associate at a shoe store. I was 26 years old, and the store manager with whom I interviewed said he believed I could be running my own store within a year. He saw something in me that I was only beginning to recognize in myself, and it was the first time someone noticed my leadership potential. I took the chance and ran with it, but when I started supervising teams in the store, I wanted everyone to be doing everything. For a while, I wouldn't budge, and my coworkers quickly became frustrated. Then I began noticing that some of my colleagues excelled at tasks such as counting inventory and merchandising apparel, while others loved being on the floor and engaging with customers. Once I began maximizing everyone's strengths by placing them where they could utilize their gifts, they were happier, I was happier, and the store was more productive. I adapted—and within a year, I was running my own store as a manager, and I saw that I could be a leader of others.

Every piece of a puzzle is different, but they all fit together to form a beautiful picture. No matter what the size of a puzzle, if you neglect a piece or try to force it to fit where it doesn't belong, the image will be distorted. It's only when the pieces are placed where they belong, each one doing what it was created to do, that the picture will come together.

> As the Bible affirms, *From him the whole body, joined and held together by every supporting ligament, grows and builds itself up in love, as each part does its work.* (Ephesians 4:16)

2. Building momentum. As young leaders, I'm convinced you and your team can do anything—but you usually can't do it all at once. Yet as you start moving forward, you will gain momentum. You often hear the term from athletes or analysts during sports contests as they describe a team having a "momentum swing" in their favor when something positive happens to change the direction of the game. It's happened because they are now heading toward the goal of winning the matchup.

So how do you begin advancing? What can you do to get the ball rolling? If it's that class project I mentioned earlier, you write up the script for your scene and read it to your two chosen friends, getting them familiar with the project and excited about taking part in it. Then, once you have their commitment, you celebrate that success, perhaps by going out to lunch together, before working on the next step of scheduling and doing the shoot itself. All of a sudden, the execution of that next step looks a little less daunting because you've built momentum.

As you are building momentum, be encouraged. You can do all things through Christ who strengthens you (Philippians 4:13). Be confident, for He who began a good work in you "will carry it on to completion until the day of Christ Jesus." (Philippians 1:6) God will give you anything you ask for according to His will (John 14:14). If you enter into agreement with the Lord, He is always faithful. But remember, faith without works is dead (James 2:26). You must execute. Do not just hear God's Word. Do it (James 1:22).

S.P.A.C.E.

You can achieve anything you want—all you have to do is create the **S.P.A.C.E.** for it. Space is an acronym that represents five powerful qualities. In order to reap the fruit of the vision God shows us, we must sow accordingly. As you create S.P.A.C.E for your destiny, you will sow intention and action. Each quality is based on wisdom from the book of Proverbs written by King Solomon, the wisest man to ever walk the planet.

1. Say it. *The tongue has the power of life and death, and those who love it will eat its fruit.* (Proverbs 18:21) You set things into motion with your words. You can use them to build or to destroy. You must speak words of life to yourself and to your team.

2. Plan it. *The plans of the diligent lead to profit as surely as haste leads to poverty.* (Proverbs 21:5) Start with the end in mind. Take the time to map out the steps needed to achieve your goal. As you write it down, other things are exposed that you may not have thought of when you first cast the vision.

3. Assess it. *Listen to advice and accept discipline, and at the end you will be counted among the wise.* (Proverbs 19:20) You can't build the roof until you build the walls, and you can't build the walls until you lay the foundation. What are the potential obstacles in front of you? What are the things you already have? What do you need to acquire? What things depend on others to be completed?

4. Commit to it. *Commit to the Lord whatever you do, and he will establish your plans.* (Proverbs 16:3) Commitment is the choice to start and the courage to keep going. Make a promise to yourself and your team that you will not let anything stop you from achieving your goal.

5. Execute it. *Many are the plans in a person's heart, but it is the Lord's purpose that prevails.* (Proverbs 19:21) If God is for you, who can be against you? Life happens at the level of events. Just do it.

Dear God, you are all knowing, all present, and all powerful. I am your child and I am becoming the leader you created me to be. As you develop me, you are providing everything that I need. Your plans and your timing are perfect in every way. You are always with me, and you are always faithful to me. Your Spirit does not make me timid, but it gives me power, love, and self-discipline. You have made me a fortified city, an iron pillar, and a bronze wall to stand against darkness, wickedness, and evil. No matter what obstacles I face, I will overcome them because greater are you who is in me than he who is in the world. Now to you who are able to keep me from stumbling and to present me before your glorious presence without fault and with great joy—to the only God my Savior be glory, majesty, power, and authority through Jesus Christ my Lord, before all time, now and forevermore! Amen.

4

PATIENCE

He has shown you, O mortal, what is good.
And what does the Lord require of you?
To act justly and to love mercy
and to walk humbly with your God.

(MICAH 6:8)

Take the time it takes, and it will take less time.

Patience is the capacity to accept or tolerate delay, trouble, or suffering without getting upset or angry. A lot of people don't want to talk about it, but patience is invaluable. The fact is, along the road to your destiny, there will be many obstacles. But be encouraged, if you are patient, then you will also see many solutions. Your ability to change what's going on around you begins with changing what's going on inside of you. You must first examine yourself to find where you need to improve, and then turn away from problematic behavior and non-productive thinking. The Good Brothers Foundation promotes a lifestyle of patience, introspection, and willingness to change. We *take the time it takes* and allow the process of growth to produce its good work in us.

49

Think of farmers who wait for the early and late rains before the precious, seeded soil produces its harvest (James 5:7). They must give themselves over to a slow, cyclical process to see their crops come to maturity. If they don't, the food they produce will be unfit for consumption. In the same way, you must patiently surrender yourself to the process of growth in order to overcome the obstacles of your destiny. Patience is the place between setting a goal and accomplishing it.

> Patience is the place between setting a goal and accomplishing it.

Before I understood the truth about patience, the thought of it made me cringe, but over the years I have developed an appreciation for these powerful points of patience.

- **Patience is provision.** In the beginning, you will not have everything you need to complete your journey, but you will have what you need to get started. If you are faithful with what you have and continue to move forward, you will find all that you need along the way.
- **Patience is power.** Mastering it allows you to have peace during your process. Anxiety is replaced with serenity, knowing that you have done what God called you to do.
- **Patience is timing.** It waits for the right time to act using the right principles in the right way.
- **Patience is achievement.** The acronym for "Good" in Good Brothers is Growing to Overcome the Obstacles of our Destiny. With patience and consistency, you will grow to overcome the obstacles of your destiny through exploration and adaptation.
- **Patience is practiced.** You don't just ask for patience and then wake up the next morning filled with it. It's

not something you can just download like an app on your phone. Instead, patience is fueled by faith.

The Bible says,

Now faith is confidence in what we hope for and assurance about what we do not see. (Hebrews 11:1)

It's drawing nearer to where you are going rather than being held back by where you are. It doesn't matter where you've been. All that matters is where you are going. You may not be there yet, but you press forward because you are confident that He who began a good work in you will carry it on to completion (Philippians 1:6). You recognize that you're further along today than you were yesterday, and you choose to live with joy in the process.

James 1:2-4 tells us, *Consider it pure joy, my brothers and sisters, whenever you face trials of many kinds, because you know that the testing of your faith produces perseverance. Let perseverance finish its work so that you may be mature and complete, not lacking anything.*

As I was writing this book, I had to be patient. I had to surrender to the very process of growth that I teach. I knew that part of my destiny was to build an international, nongovernmental organization that served to transform the way young men think. To achieve the goal God placed on my heart, I had to accept that patience was the place between my vision and the realization of my destiny.

When I talk about patience and faith, I would be remiss if I did not discuss their chief adversary: worry. You probably struggle with worry far more than you should. I know that was my experience in my teen and young adult years. In college, I served as a resident assistant (RA). In that role, I operated as a liaison between the school and the students in my dormitory. In return, I received free housing, a book stipend, and an all-you-can-eat meal plan. It was a great gig. My role required me to interact with people all over campus as well as plan events at my building to facilitate relationships among the residents.

While I was carrying out that role, I decided to pledge for a fraternity. As we began the initiation process, my line (pledge class) and I were placed on social probation, a restriction during which there were limits on who we could talk to and the events we could participate in on campus. As a new initiate, I was worried that if I violated social probation, I would be dropped from the line. I should have been patient and thought things through, but I let worry guide my decision about how to overcome the obstacle I was facing. I ended up severely neglecting my responsibilities because I didn't take the time to clarify what I was and wasn't allowed to do in relation to my RA duties while on social probation.

When my initiation period ended, I was given a choice: either resign from the RA job or go on probation with the school to make up for the work I had missed. I decided to resign because I was worried that I wouldn't be able to repair the damage on the job and manage my fraternity involvement at the same time.

As a result, I not only forfeited my job, but I ended up going further into debt to pay for housing. Instead of patiently taking the time to examine my options, I wasted the benefits I had enjoyed as an RA. Had I been patient and thought it through, I would have made an entirely different decision.

Your battle with worry and patience may be different. Let's say you have schoolwork due. You have to turn in a paper, study for a test, attend an event with a friend, and go to work—all in the next 24 hours. You're overwhelmed with anxiety to the point you don't feel like you can do anything. You know you need to keep your responsibilities. What do you do?

Explore and adapt. You find a solution. In this case, you decide the non-negotiable task is work, if for no other reason because you can't afford to not earn the income. The event with your friend? Well, it lasts two hours, but if you're there for part of it, you can leave early. That leaves the paper and the test. In the time remaining, you know you cannot do both.

You think about it and decide doing well on the test is more crucial to your grade in class than being penalized for not getting the paper done on time. So, you study for the test and email the professor about the paper, asking for an extension. Because you own up to your mistake and are prepared to accept the consequences of turning the paper in late, even if it means getting a lesser grade, the professor grants you the extension. You pass the test with a B+ and end up getting a C for a paper you know was good enough for an A. Nicely done! You completed all your tasks and kept all your commitments. You also learned a valuable lesson about time management you can use in the future.

■ — — ■

I once learned a saying from one of my friends. It went something like this: "I have only just a minute, only 60 seconds in it. Forced upon me, can't refuse it. Didn't seek it, didn't choose it. But it's up to me to use it. Give account if I abuse it. I have only just a minute, but eternity is in it." You must do the best you can with what you have. What's the use of wasting time worrying that your plan is not going to work when you can be using that same time to get closer to your goals?

We're going to be faced with various problems and solutions every day. If the problem has a solution, there is *no need* to worry. Likewise, if the problem does not have a solution, there is *no point* to worrying. Any problematic situation basically ends one of two ways. Either you discover the solution and restore harmony—or there is no solution, and you have to accept the situation, reset your thinking, and explore new avenues to adaptation. That's what The Good Brothers Foundation is all about. Worry has no place in your mind, and in the end, you gain nothing from it anyway.

A Bible passage asks, *Can any one of you by worrying add a single hour to your life?* (Matthew 6:27)

The answer is no. Worry doesn't get you any closer to where you need to be, and it causes you to think more about what is *not* going to work rather than what *is* going to work.

After college, while working at my full-time job, I started to realize I wanted to do more. I was recruiting and training employees, and I had a message about life and leadership that was bigger than retail. I was succeeding in the company, but I felt like a caged bird. I wanted to fly.

I had a friend in Arizona who told me about an opportunity that would allow me to use the skills I had developed in retail—sales, management, and leadership—to become an entrepreneur. He explained there was no limit to the earning potential. My plan was to work with him, save more money, and then use that money to do what I wanted to do (and what has ended up becoming The Good Brothers Foundation).

After several months of planning and preparation, it was time to move to Tucson, Arizona. My parents were sad about me leaving home, but they were supportive, as were my co-workers. After driving cross-country, I went to work with my friend in his company.

He and I had known each other for a long time and got along very well. It started off great, and I began working toward my goals.

Again, I did well, but after a while that same caged-bird feeling set in again. I had to continue to search and find what I wanted—but I sensed that would mean staying in Arizona. I left that job, took the money I had saved, paid my rent several months in advance, and started volunteering and serving around the city. I got involved in a city transformation organization called 4Tucson with their NextGen initiative. I joined the Arizona Christian Men's Fellowship and stepped into leadership roles there. I volunteered with Prison Fellowship and at the Bridge Home, a faith-based transitional home for men coming out of incarceration. I even served at the city mayor's office to support the mentorship programs in the city. I jumped right in—and those opportunities then led to other roles, including a paid position at Boys to Men, where I was able to gain specialized experience and education while earning income to start my own business. I met my brilliant wife, got my minister's license, and eventually planted a church. If you keep moving toward your goal, then doors will open for you.

> If you keep moving toward your goal, then doors will open for you.

Like my mother always said, "If you *take the time it takes*, it will take less time." A lot of people don't see patience this way because we live in a culture of instant gratification. We are tempted to take shortcuts and end up having to double back when we would have saved time by just doing it right from the beginning. Remember, growth is a process—and it takes time.

Dear God, you are my provider. You are making and
will make provision for all that you have planned for me in
due season. You said that what I bind on earth will be bound
in heaven, and so I bind the spirit of worry and anxiety in
the name of Jesus. I loose faith, blessed confidence in what
I hope for and assurance about what I do not see, in Jesus'
name. I will consider it pure joy whenever I face trials of
many kinds, because I know that the testing of my faith
produces perseverance. Not by my might, nor by my power,
but by your spirit, perseverance will finish its work
so that I may be mature and complete, not lacking
anything. In Jesus' name, Amen.

5

GOOD BROTHERS

But you are a chosen people, a royal priesthood, a holy nation,
God's special possession, that you may declare the praises of him
who called you out of darkness into his wonderful light.

(1 PETER 2:9)

Do it for the culture.

Culture is broken down into three things: beliefs, traditions, and values. You can create whatever culture you want based on the beliefs, traditions, and values you have in common with a group of people.

Beliefs speak to what you trust in and confidently accept to be true. This is where faith comes into play. Traditions are practices, activities, or behaviors learned from the group(s) you associate with. Values are principles and standards that indicate your judgments about what is important in life. Values are what you care about.

These three vital things create *what* you do, *how* you do it, and *why* you do it—and they define the culture in you that you then manifest to others around you. As a young leader, the culture you create directly impacts your ability to achieve your shared mission.

When some people consider culture, their first thoughts go to race and skin color, but that is flawed thinking. Regardless of the color of your skin, we are all of one race: humanity. The Bible teaches us that God created all of us from one man.

> *From one man he made all the nations, that they should inhabit the whole earth; and he marked out their appointed times in history and the boundaries of their lands. God did this so that they would seek him and perhaps reach out for him and find him, though he is not far from any one of us.* (Acts 17:26-27)

I believe every person is connected. Within this one race, there are cultures, groups of people who share common beliefs, traditions, and values. When we discriminate because of the skin color of another person, we are using a decidedly incomplete basis for our judgment. As Dr. King so eloquently taught us, we should only judge another person according to the content of their character.

DEALING WITH DISCRIMINATION

If you have faced, or ever do face, discrimination, the proper response begins with perspective. Understand that it is the discriminatory person, not you, who is flawed. Do not allow yourself to take a victim mentality. Next, be determined to pursue your mission regardless of what others think of you or even do against you. Your drive is what will keep you going, and that resilience and grit comes from within. It can never be taken away from you, so you must be careful not to forfeit

> "Better to light a candle than to curse the darkness."

it. Allow your determination to cause you to withstand any obstacle that comes against you. Lastly, you are to shine in the midst of the discrimination. An old Chinese proverb states, "Better to light a candle than to curse the darkness." Accepting the reality of the discrimination does not give permission to it; rather, acceptance creates the space for exploration and adaptation. Mahatma Ghandi, the renowned leader of India's independence movement against British rule, exhorted, "Be the change that you wish to see in the world." That is the proper response to discrimination. Understand it, keep on marching, and do not perpetuate it.

■ — — ■

For me, the most important part of culture is the **"why,"** which comes from my faith. As I'm sure you've guessed by now, I am a Christian. I trust in God and confidently accept Him to be true. My faith is predicated on my relationship with the person and teachings of Jesus Christ. For you, it may be a different religion. The major world religions, in order of estimated followers after Christianity (31.5 percent), are Islam (23.2 percent), Hinduism (15 percent), and Buddhism (7.1 percent).[10] Islam is the religion of the Muslims, a monotheistic faith regarded as revealed through Muhammad as the Prophet of Allah. Hinduism is a major religious and cultural tradition of South Asia that has many gods and teaches that people have another life on earth after they die via reincarnation. Buddhism is a religion of eastern and central Asia that grew out of the teachings of Siddhartha Gautama, who said people can be liberated from suffering by cultivating wisdom, virtue, and concentration.

While the tenets and practices of these religions have little in common, what holds them all together is how they make us multicultural as a human race. There is an innate desire in each one of us to be connected to a greater purpose while simultaneously belonging with one another. Through your chosen beliefs and the faith they foster, you are invited to make a personal transformation that empowers you to build on and personify the culture that you are connected to.

GOOD BROTHERS' CULTURE

The Good Brothers Foundation exists to transform the way young men think. We know that when we change our thinking and choose to grow, then we can change our lives. We are committed to growing to overcome the obstacles of our destiny. Our mission is to help young men live intentional lives and become the leaders God created them to be. We follow a Bible-based and Christ-centered ethic to inform our culture.

So, what are the Christian beliefs, traditions, and values we draw from to create this culture?

- Beliefs: *There is one body and one Spirit, just as you were called to one hope when you were called; one Lord, one faith, one baptism; one God and Father of all, who is over all and through all and in all.* (Ephesians 4:4-6)
- Values: *"Love the Lord your God with all your heart and with all your soul and with all your mind." This is the first and greatest commandment. And the second is like it: "Love your neighbor as yourself."* (Matthew 22:37-39)
- Traditions: *Then Jesus came to them and said, "All authority in heaven and on earth has been given to me. Therefore go and make disciples of all nations, baptizing them in the name of the Father and of the Son and of the Holy Spirit, and teaching them to obey everything I have commanded you. And surely I am with you always, to the very end of the age."* (Matthew 28:18-20)

GOOD BROTHERS

The Bible teaches that God has laid two paths before us, one of curse and another of blessing.

> *This day I call the heavens and the earth as witnesses against you that I have set before you life and death, blessings and curses. Now choose life, so that you and your children may live.* (Deuteronomy 30:19)

It is up to each man which path he will choose, a freedom that requires us, as Good Brothers, to give others the respect to make their choice, knowing God will hold us all accountable for our decisions in due time.

We guide our behavior using these ten sayings:

1. *Do the right thing*
Adhere to the codes of conduct as they pertain to the schools, communities, cities, and nations we serve.

2. *The cup is half full*
Focus on opportunities rather than obstacles as we work to achieve our goals.

3. *Choose to grow*
Seek first to understand and then be understood.

4. *We are family*
Stick together through good times and bad, learning together and serving together.

5. *Be the change*
"Well done" is better than "well said."

6. *I am my brothers' keeper*
Do unto others as you would have done unto you.

7. *Don't take it personal*
Our process does not change people; it changes thinking. People change themselves. Focus on the process.

8. *Greatest good for the greatest number*
Operate with consistent availability and boundaries of service for all who we serve. If they want what we have, and they are willing to do what it takes to obtain it, then it will be theirs.

9. *Smile*
No pain lasts forever.

10. *The show must go on*
Good Brothers is fair. Good Brothers is hard. Good Brothers is not for everyone.

■·—·—·■

As the founder, I am responsible for teaching and modeling our culture. As a leader among brothers, I am also charged with the duty of guiding, protecting, and settling disputes. In this way, my goal is to lead the brothers into a strategy for a fulfilling, Christ-centered life. I will carry out these roles faithfully and with a father's heart.

This is my pledge, establishing and defining who I am as a leader.

"By God's infinite grace and mercy, I will support and defend the Holy Bible against all enemies, foreign and domestic. I will bear true faith and allegiance to the same. I take this obligation freely, without any mental reservation or purpose of evasion. I will well and earnestly perform the duties of the office I occupy. I will administer truth and justice without respect to persons and do equal right to the poor and to the rich. I will faithfully and impartially discharge all the duties incumbent upon me in accordance with the Word of God and under the direction of the Holy Spirit. In Jesus' name, Amen."

God has given us all the gifts that we need through Jesus Christ. We are one body with many functioning parts. Working together as a body, we maximize our gifts to glorify the Father and benefit the body. Finally, as Good Brothers, we charge one another with duties pertaining to the following seven key areas:

1. **Membership**: *Be a present member of a church.*
   - Exercise your gifts and abilities in the church for the betterment of God's people and in support of what He is doing through that assembly
   - Give financially to the church through tithes and offerings
   - Participate in events hosted by the church and invite people to attend

2. **Brotherhood:** *View yourself as a servant leader.*
   - Keep the bond of peace between men in the church
   - Work in unity with the leaders of the church
   - Serve and protect the women and children of the church

3. **Athleticism:** *Put forth your best effort to meet the needs of the church.*
   - Take care of your body, God's temple
   - Exercise regularly
   - Eat healthy

4. **Community:** *The whole is greater than the sum of its parts.*
   - Work together as a unit
   - Be vision oriented
   - Maximize each person's strengths

5. **Discipline:** *Do things in a fitting and orderly way*
   - Operate in obedience to your Heavenly Father
   - Maintain your integrity
   - Exercise self-control

6. **Self-sacrifice:** *It's not sacrifice until it feels like it.*
   - Lay down your own will and pick up the will of God
   - Do what is the greatest thing for the group
   - Do what will glorify God

7. **Devotion:** *Dedicate your time, abilities, resources, and thoughts to God.*
   - Read your bible daily
   - Pray without ceasing
   - Worship God with what you say, what you do, and what you have

CONFLICT RESOLUTION

We will deal with conflict through restorative practices. Conflict is inevitable, but growth from conflict is optional—and we choose to grow by being a conduit of healing for one another. Conflict arises out of hurt, whether it's hurt that we've perpetrated on another person or hurt that has been inflicted upon us. We forgive one another as we have been forgiven by our Heavenly Father. Whatever the infraction, we will not shame one another, but we will address the behavior and seek to be reconciled and restored. We create a safe space to discuss what happened, how we were affected, and what should be done to repair the harm. This is a process of restorative justice. We do all this to bring each other back into alignment with our culture, first as a family of faith, then as Good Brothers.

Dear God, you are the Father of all. The true and living God. Teach me how to live peacefully with others in accordance with your plans and purposes. The devil tries to turn me against them, but I am no longer a slave to sin. Hallelujah! I am dead to sin and alive to God in Christ Jesus. How good and pleasant it is when brothers live together in unity! Grace and peace be to the brothers from God the Father and the Lord Jesus Christ. Let the love of the brothers continue. Bind us together, oh God, by your Spirit. Then we will be harmonious, sympathetic, brotherly, kindhearted, and humble in spirit toward one another. We will honor all people, love the brotherhood, fear God, and respect our leaders. In the name of Jesus Christ, Amen.

6

BECOMING
A GODLY MAN

Do not conform to the pattern of this world, but be transformed
by the renewing of your mind. Then you will be able to test and
approve what God's will is—his good, pleasing and perfect will.
(ROMANS 12:2)

A part of society,
but apart from it.

The Bible tells us that God created mankind in His own image as male and female (Genesis 1:27). Yet being born a male doesn't make you a man. To become the man God created you to be, you have to discover the roles and responsibilities of a man in the Kingdom of God, and then learn how to fulfill them.

Roles and responsibilities are paramount because everything in the Kingdom of God is done decently and in order (1 Corinthians 14:40). We see roles and responsibilities carried out everywhere. In the classroom, for example, it is the teacher's responsibility to prepare a lesson plan, have the necessary materials, and to help facilitate learning. The student's responsibility is to pay attention, go through the worksheets and the exercises, and ask questions when they are unclear. When this relationship happens in proper order, roles are fulfilled: the teacher is able to teach, and the student is able to learn.

In a professional setting, if someone wants start a business, his responsibility is to identify where there is a need and come up with a solution, test his service/product to make sure it works well and fills that need, and then get the information out about his service/product to those with the need. He will also seek and find different people to manage his business—customer service, marketing, and manufacturing—each one with their own set of roles and responsibilities.

On a football team, the players are primarily divided into offense and defense. Each squad has a job to do. The offense needs to advance the ball down the field and score. The defense needs to protect their territory, shut down the opponents' plays, and stop the ball from getting to the end zone. There are other groups, such as special teams or the practice squad, whose players have specific roles and responsibilities to fulfill, even if they rarely get on the field during a game.

So much of what society tells us about manhood is false. The lies originated with Satan. His goal is to usher in a state of confusion and hinder men from being who God created them to be. If you are not careful to reject Satan's lies and deception, then you will be tempted to forget who you are.

James admonishes us to *not merely listen to the word, and so deceive yourselves. Do what it says. Anyone who listens to the word but does not do what it says is like someone who looks at his face in a mirror and, after looking at himself, goes away and immediately forgets what he looks like.*

But whoever looks intently into the perfect law that gives freedom and continues in it—not forgetting what they have heard, but doing it—they will be blessed in what they do. (James 1:22-25)

Every lie that Satan tells is part of his evil scheme "to steal and kill and destroy" us (John 10:10). He knows that in God you are unstoppable, so his goal is to prevent you from moving in the power, love, and self-control God intends for you (1 Timothy 1:7). Becoming a Godly man requires you to accept that God defines you, not society. You must walk by faith and not by sight (2 Corinthians 5:7) so that your identity

> Becoming a Godly man requires you to accept that God defines you, not society.

is determined by submission to divine authority rather than succumbing to a sinful society. You are warned in 1 John 2:15-17:

Do not love the world or anything in the world. If anyone loves the world, love for the Father is not in them. For everything in the world—the lust of the flesh, the lust of the eyes, and the pride of life—comes not from the Father but from the world. The world and its desires pass away, but whoever does the will of God lives forever.

Lies that society tells about how to be a man include:

1. You must be powerful and dominating.
2. You must be fearless and in control.
3. You must be strong and emotionless.
4. You must be successful by any means necessary: in the boardroom, the bedroom, and on the ball field.

Your power is accessed through obedience to God. Ephesians 6:12 declares that his battle:

> "is not against flesh and blood, but against the rulers, against the authorities, against the powers of this dark world and against the spiritual forces of evil in the heavenly realms."

Dominion is yours; therefore, you do not have to dominate. If you feel like you must dominate, then in that moment, you have forgotten your identity in Christ.

Godly men treat God with respect and honor. We place our trust in Him as the one from whom all provision and protection flows. We acknowledge Him as the one who is in control of all things on earth and in heaven. We are careful to do everything we can to glorify Him by making decisions based on His Word.

Being a Godly man is not about being emotionless, but it is about managing your emotions and channeling them into positive words and actions. Emotions are part of who you are, but if you do not handle them, then they will handle you! Seek God for wisdom about your emotions—for when you rely on Him, nothing can break you. Romans 8:38-39 declares:

> *For I am convinced that neither death nor life, neither angels nor demons, neither the present nor the future, nor any powers, neither height nor depth, nor anything else in all creation, will be able to separate us from the love of God that is in Christ Jesus our Lord.*

Your success is not determined by this sinful society's standards, which have been saturated with deceit from Satan. In the boardroom, you are ethical and honest leaders who do everything with excellence and integrity. In the bedroom, you view your sexual relationship with your wife as an act of worship to God done with honor toward one another. On the field, you play with sportsmanship, respecting coaches, teammates, opponents, and fans alike.

Troy Vincent said, "Life is about focus, life is about structure, and life is about accountability." When we accept that God is the greatest authority and decide to make pleasing Him our focus, then we can live the lives we were created to live. As 1 Corinthians 13:11 teaches:

> When I was a child, I talked like a child, I thought like a child, I reasoned like a child. When I became a man, I put the ways of childhood behind me.

God created you with specific plans and purposes for your relationships, your soul, your character, your ministry, and your personal disciplines. When you do what He teaches you to do, you will be in alignment with who you are supposed to be. Former National Football League quarterback Jon Kitna said, "You + God = Enough." To understand how you can become the man you were created to be, you have to go back to the beginning of all mankind, "in his own image, in the image of God he created them; male and female He created them." (Genesis 1:27) As creations of the Creator, there-

"You + God = Enough."

fore, "in him we live and move and have our being," (Acts 17:28) and as men in the Kingdom of God, we have roles and responsibilities: first to God, then to your family, your church, and your school or work. There are six primary roles and responsibilities every man must learn how to fill.

1. Provider
2. Protector
3. Teacher
4. Cultivator
5. Visionary
6. Leader

Before we look at each one in more detail, recognize that as Good Brothers we first and foremost rely on God to be all of those things *for us.* In turn, we serve in those roles and responsibilities alongside our fellow brothers on behalf of others, particularly the women and children in our lives. We also understand that they will count on us to meet these roles and responsibilities physically, mentally, and spiritually.

The roles and responsibilities of men and women are equally valuable, but each were created by God to play different parts. The Lord designed women to come alongside the man to give and nurture life within the family as a mother and wife. She encourages the growth and development of the culture that is being taught in the home, serving as both a first-follower and the right hand in the nurturing of those beliefs, values, and traditions. The woman also enhances the visionary and leadership roles of a man, improving and intensifying each role by holding boundaries and ensuring that the man stays on course and does not go astray. She expands the vision by creating experiences that both support and add to the vision in a way that brings it to new life for the family.

Children, too, have the responsibility declared by Scripture to honor their father and mother (Exodus 20:12, Ephesians 6:2). Just as we earlier looked at balance being a noun and a verb, the same is true of honor. Children are to have high respect and esteem for their parents (noun) while respecting and fulfilling their obligations toward and agreements with their mother and father (verb). As they do, the Bible says things will go well for them and that they will enjoy long life (Deuteronomy 5:16, Ephesians 6:3).

Together, whether it's in our families or within the teams we lead, we must be willing and able to step up and do whatever needs to be done in our roles and responsibilities so that everything can flow as smoothly as possible. Here is a deeper look at each of the roles and responsibilities you are to fulfill as a man.

Provider: Provide for both tangible and intangible needs. While providing—money, food, shelter, and clothing—we also provide love and support through our words and actions.

Protector: Protect from natural danger and from spiritual darkness. We mediate and settle quarrels, fostering caring, positive interactions. We pray for ourselves and others.

Teacher: Teach about God, His Kingdom, and our faith. Instruct about worldly systems and people. We help others discover and develop their gifts.

Cultivator: Cultivate people by establishing expectations and holding boundaries. Prepare others to make positive contributions to family, church, workplace, and community.

Visionary: We hold a far-sighted hope of a positive outcome for ourselves and those around us. We communicate this hope prophetically, consistently, and confidently.

Leader: We model what it is that we expect. Our responsibility is to show up, be the head, and stay the course.

■ — — ■

Pastor, speaker, and author Tony Evans said, "You can be a male and not be a man. Malehood has to do with your biological gender. Manhood has to do with submission to your divine authority." Becoming a Godly man means making Jesus Christ the *Lord* of your attitude, priorities, health, family, thinking, commitment, faith, relationships, values, growth, finances, and generosity. When you follow Jesus, He will lead you into peace, power, positivity, and purity. Only He can teach you how to be a true man—a Godly man. As Jesus said:

I am the way and the truth and the life. No one comes to the Father except through me. (John 14:6)

The Word of God teaches things differently than the world does. You must reject what society tries to project on you. By holding yourself and others accountable to God's Word, you are breaking up the soil in preparation to receive new life so that together we can accomplish His purposes. God created you to operate under His control, reflect His power, and trust His love to direct and preserve you.

Dear God, you are my banner. You created me in your own image; therefore, in order to become the man you created me to be, I must submit to your divine authority. Thank you for guiding and protecting me on my journey to and through manhood. When I was a child, I talked like a child, I thought like a child, I reasoned like a child. When I became a man, I put the ways of childhood behind me. My struggle is not against flesh and blood, but against the rulers, against the authorities, against the powers of this dark world, and against the spiritual forces of evil in the heavenly realms. I place my hope in you, Lord, and you will renew my strength. I will soar on wings like eagles. I will run and not grow weary. I will walk and not be faint, being confident of this: that *you* who began a good work in me will carry it on to completion. In Jesus' name, Amen.

7

CREATING A LEGACY

For the grace of God has appeared that offers salvation to all people. It teaches us to say "No" to ungodliness and worldly passions, and to live self-controlled, upright and godly lives in this present age, while we wait for the blessed hope—the appearing of the glory of our great God and Savior, Jesus Christ, who gave himself for us to redeem us from all wickedness and to purify for himself a people that are his very own, eager to do what is good. These, then, are the things you should teach. Encourage and rebuke with all authority. Do not let anyone despise you.

(TITUS 2:11-15)

Be faithful.

I'm proud of you. Every moment of every day, you are growing something into reality—at work or at school, in your relationships or in yourself. You are purposeful in your present and forward thinking about your future.

The fact that you even picked up this book, let alone finished it, is a testament to your awareness and desire to grow. I don't take that lightly. As a young man, you are in charge of your own life. You will face obstacles, but whether they are internal or external, you will grow to overcome them. This mindset, defined as a determination to grow to overcome the obstacles of your destiny, is what The Good Brothers Foundation is devoted to spreading. Whether you thought about it like that or not, that's exactly what you are doing: growing to overcome the obstacles of your destiny. You were created to leave a powerful legacy. You have a divine calling to work with others toward accomplishing a common goal, and you will do this by building relationships and solving problems using biblical solutions.

> You were created to leave a powerful legacy.

The ugly side to this truth is that you also have an enemy, Satan, who is devoted to keeping you from fulfilling your destiny. He has a clearly defined, three-tiered objective revealed in John 10:10. It says, "The thief comes only to steal and kill and destroy." But don't worry. This enemy is a defeated foe. He knows it. Still, hoping that you are not convinced of that truth, Satan will do whatever he can to deter you from accomplishing what God created you to do. For this very reason, you are constantly exploring your opportunities for growth. Even more, you pray and ask God to search your heart and correct you so that you can turn away from problematic behavior and non-productive thinking. Practicing justice and doing what is right will strengthen you, your team, and your family.

That said, developing a lifestyle of genuine introspection and determination to change for the better doesn't happen overnight. You must follow my mother's adage. "If you *take the time it takes*, it will take less time." Such a demand requires discipline, leadership, and patience to allow the process to produce its good work in you. Without commitment to a steady, long-term personal investment in the things of God, you will not realize your potential.

Life is all about choices. When I was a child, my mother taught me that the only person I have control of is myself. As I became a man, God taught me that when I'm not intentional about moving toward Him, I am going away from Him. He showed me how my beliefs are the foundation for what I trust and confidently accept to be true. Your values are the principles and standards that influence your decisions. They determine what you do, how you do it, and why you do what you do. They define the culture you manifest for others around you. As a young leader, the culture you create directly impacts and informs the people around you. When you allow ungodly influences to direct your decisions, their impact is injurious to your growth and damaging to the impact you have on others. Left unchecked, these evil influences will wreak havoc on your life as a man and lead you, your team, and your family down a path to destruction.

You understand the importance of being intentional. You are powerful. Your power comes from God, and with that power comes instruction on how to wield it with meekness, confidence, and consistency. You are humble and seek to please God through obedience. You do what is right in His sight, not in your own eyes, so your success is not measured by society's values. You properly appropriate your fear by placing your trust in God as the One from whom all blessings flow and who has control of all things. You rest in Him and rely on His precepts and truths so that nothing can break you. Each man has the power to create his own legacy. As part of The Good Brothers Foundation , are part of a greater legacy: that of the Father, the Son, and the Holy Spirit. Your inheritance is victory. You are a remnant of those who went before you, and a beacon to those who will follow.

You live by the biblical mandate to:

TAKE THE TIME IT TAKES

Trust in the Lord with all your heart and lean not on your own understanding; in all your ways submit to him, and he will make your paths straight. (Proverbs 3:5-6)

You realize that when you operate in this fashion, you align your influence on others with the effect God's Word has had on you. You accept the responsibility you have as a man of God to create an impression on others that reflects the Bible and its truths. You know that this is the only way to have an eternal impact on those around you, and you understand that living and declaring God's Word is the only way you will grow to overcome the obstacles of your destiny.

Dear God, you created the universe and everything in it. In you I live and move and have my being. For by grace I have been saved through faith, and that not of myself, it is the gift from you, God, not of works, lest anyone should boast. For I am your workmanship, created in Christ Jesus for good works which you prepared beforehand that I should walk in them. Thank you! You called me out of darkness into your wonderful light. I am a chosen people, a royal priesthood, a holy nation, your special possession, Father, that I may declare your praises! I am a remnant of the good brothers who have gone before me, and a beacon to those that will follow. Teach me to do your will, for you are my God. Let your good Spirit lead me on level ground. By your Spirit, I will be on your guard and stand firm in the faith. By your grace and your mercy, I will be courageous and strong. I will leave the legacy that you have created me to leave: your will, your way, your results. I bless you, and I praise you. Now to the King eternal, immortal, invisible, the only God, be honor and glory forever and ever. In the name of Jesus Christ I pray, Amen and Amen.

EPILOGUE

This is what the Lord says:

> *Cursed is the one who trusts in man, who draws strength from mere flesh and whose heart turns away from the Lord. That person will be like a bush in the wastelands; they will not see prosperity when it comes. They will dwell in the parched places of the desert, in a salt land where no one lives.*
>
> *But blessed is the one who trusts in the Lord, whose confidence is in him. They will be like a tree planted by the water that sends out its roots by the stream. It does not fear when heat comes; its leaves are always green. It has no worries in a year of drought and never fails to bear fruit.*
>
> (JEREMIAH 17:5-8)

I wrote this book because I care about you. The stories and concepts I share have shaped and transformed my life. Just know that the most important part of this book is the Scripture. I can't give you a blueprint for life, but God's Word can.

I pray God fills you with the knowledge of His will through all the wisdom and understanding that the Spirit gives, so that you may live a life worthy of the Lord and please Him in every way. May you bear fruit in every good work and be strengthened with all power according to His glorious might, so that you may have great endurance and patience and give joyful thanks to the Father, who has qualified you to share in the inheritance of His holy people in the Kingdom of light. In the matchless, marvelous, and majestic name of Jesus Christ I pray, Amen.

STAY CONNECTED

**Visit
www.TheGoodBrothersFoundation.org**

ENDNOTES

1 Curry has a tattoo of 1 Corinthians 13:8 in Hebrew on his wrist ("Love never fails.")

2 From https://study.com/academy/lesson/what-is-physical-health -definition-components-examples.html

3 From "How long can you go without sleep?" Dr. Simon Kyle. https:// www.sleepio.com/articles/sleep-science/how-long-can-you-go -without-sleep/

4 From https://familydoctor.org/mental-health-keeping-your -emotional-health/

5 From https://www.who.int/features/factfiles/mental_health/en/

6 From https://study.com/academy/lesson/what-is-social-health -definition-examples.html

7 From https://wellness.ucr.edu/spiritual_wellness.html

8 From "What is The Law of Attraction," http://www.thelawofattraction .com/what-is-the-law-of-attraction/

9 Martin Luther King, Jr., "I Have A Dream: Writings and Speeches that Changed the World," ed. James Melvin Washington (San Francisco: Harper, 1986), 102-106.

10 The Pew Forum on Religion & Public Life, "The Global Religious Landscape," Pew Research Center. December 18, 2012.

Made in the USA
Middletown, DE
14 January 2023

21586322R00050